THIS JOURNAL BELONGS TO

_____

+

_____

DATE NIGHT IN

DATE

A Journal for Couples

NIGHT

BY Lisa Nola

ILLUSTRATED BY Camilla Perkins

IN

CHRONICLE BOOKS

SAN FRANCISCO

ISBN 978-1-4521-8389-3

Manufactured in China.

Design by Lizzie Vaughan.
Illustrations by Camilla Perkins.
Typeset in Folk, Nobel, and Cooper Black.

10 9 8 7 6 5 4 3 2

Chronicle Books publishes distinctive books and gifts. From
award-winning children's titles, bestselling cookbooks, and eclectic
pop culture to acclaimed works of art and design, stationery, and
journals, we craft publishing that's instantly recognizable for its
spirit and creativity. Enjoy our publishing and become part of our
community at www.chroniclebooks.com.

Chronicle Books LLC
680 Second Street
San Francisco, CA 94107
www.chroniclebooks.com

[PHOTO OF US]

CONTENTS

HOW DO YOU DREAM TOGETHER? HOW DO YOU REVISIT MEMORIES? HOW DO YOU MAKE EACH OTHER LAUGH? HOW DO YOU SPARK CONVERSATIONS THAT ARE UNIQUE TO JUST THE TWO OF YOU OR DISCOVER MYSTERIOUS CORNERS IN EACH OTHER'S MINDS?

YES! YOU JOURNAL TOGETHER.

SPRINKLE THIS ACTIVITY INTO YOUR DAYS TO BRING YOU A LITTLE CLOSER.

OPEN TO ANY PAGE OR START AT THE BEGINNING AND WORK YOUR WAY FORWARD. SOME PAGES YOU FILL OUT

TOGETHER. SOME PAGES YOU FILL OUT
INDIVIDUALLY AND SHARE AFTERWARD.
JUST DECIDE WHO WILL BE "A"_____
AND WHO WILL BE "B"_____. YOU
CAN JOURNAL OVER DINNER. JOURNAL
UNDER THE COVERS. BRING IT ON
VACATION. START OFF ANY DATE NIGHT
WITH JUST ONE PAGE AND SEE WHERE
IT TAKES YOU. ADD TO YOUR JOURNAL
OVER TIME, AND (VOILÀ!) YOU HAVE A
VERY SPECIAL KEEPSAKE.

STAY CONNECTED . . .
JOURNAL AND CHILL.

Lisa Nola   www.listography.com

THINGS WE'RE
GRATEFUL FOR

_____

_____

_____

_____

_____

_____

_____

_____

_____

_____

_____

COMMONALITIES AND COINCIDENCES BETWEEN US

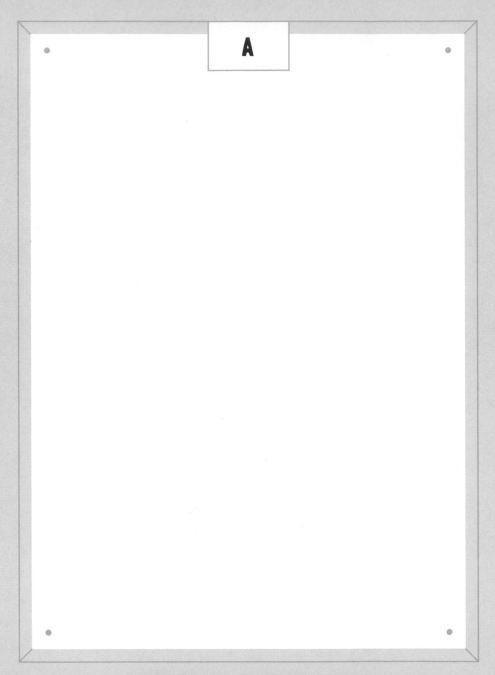

A

AMATEUR PORTRAITS

B

OF EACH OTHER

THINGS WE AGREE
TO DISAGREE ON

MOVIES OF SPECIAL
SIGNIFICANCE TO US

SONGS OF SPECIAL SIGNIFICANCE TO US

MUSIC WE'VE SEEN LIVE

A

INDIVIDUAL AND MATCHING TATTOOS

B

THAT WOULD MAKE SENSE FOR US

OUR DREAM MUSIC FESTIVAL LINEUP (DEAD OR ALIVE)

CITIES AND COUNTRIES
WE'VE VISITED

CITIES AND COUNTRIES
WE HOPE TO VISIT

☐ _____
☐ _____
☐ _____
☐ _____
☐ _____
☐ _____
☐ _____
☐ _____
☐ _____
☐ _____
☐ _____
☐ _____
☐ _____
☐ _____
☐ _____
☐ _____
☐ _____
☐ _____

☐ _____
☐ _____
☐ _____
☐ _____
☐ _____
☐ _____
☐ _____
☐ _____
☐ _____
☐ _____
☐ _____
☐ _____
☐ _____
☐ _____
☐ _____
☐ _____
☐ _____
☐ _____

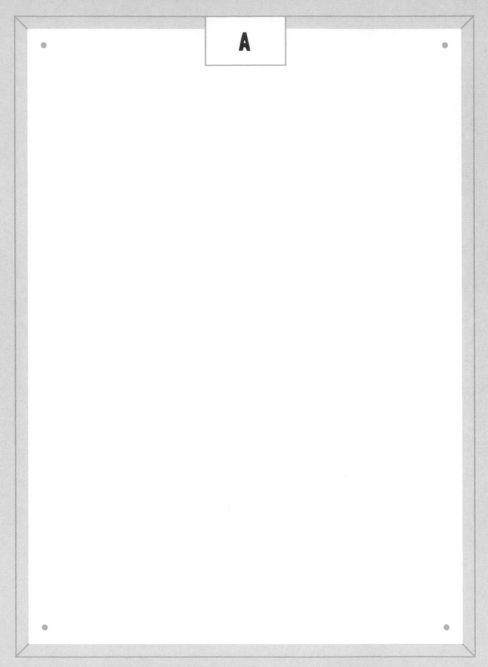

A

HOW WE'D EACH DESCRIBE

B

A PERFECT DAY TOGETHER

NATIONAL PARKS WE'VE VISITED
AND HOPE TO VISIT

VISITED

TO VISIT

FUNNY, SWEET, AND MEMORABLE THINGS WE'VE SAID TO EACH OTHER

SILLY PET PEEVES WE HAVE

A

WITH EACH OTHER

B

VOWS AND VALUES
WE THINK ARE IMPORTANT
FOR THE LONG TERM

THESE SYMBOLS WOULD APPEAR

ON OUR FAMILY CREST

GOOD STUFF THAT'S HAPPENED TO US WHILE TOGETHER

DIFFICULT STUFF THAT'S HAPPENED TO US WHILE TOGETHER

_____

_____

_____

_____

_____

_____

_____

_____

_____

_____

_____

_____

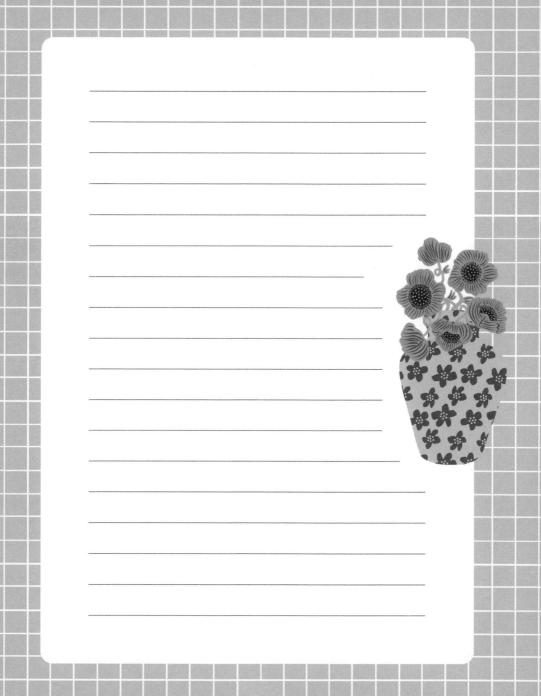

HOW WE'VE SPENT SPECIAL OCCASIONS WITH EACH OTHER

OCCASION

PLACE

_____

_____

_____

_____

_____

_____

_____

_____

_____

_____

_____

_____

_____

_____

_____

_____

_____

_____

_____

_____

_____

_____

_____

_____

"WOULD YOU RATHER . . ."

A

Be kissed on the neck or tummy?

QUIZ

B

Know when you're going to die or not know?

_____

OUR GOOD FRIENDS
AND HOW WE MET THEM

FRIEND'S NAME   **HOW WE MET**

OUR ULTIMATE DINNER PARTY GUEST LIST (REAL OR FICTIONAL)

_____   _____

_____   _____

_____   _____

_____   _____

_____   _____

_____   _____

_____   _____

_____   _____

_____   _____

_____   _____

_____   _____

OUR FAMILY MEMBERS AND
WHAT WE APPRECIATE ABOUT THEM

FAMILY MEMBER   **WHAT WE APPRECIATE**

"HOW WELL DO YOU KNOW ME?"

A

MY QUESTION	YOUR ANSWER	RIGHT!	WRONG!
What's my shoe size?		☐	☐
What was the name of my first pet?		☐	☐
		☐	☐
		☐	☐
		☐	☐
		☐	☐
		☐	☐
		☐	☐
		☐	☐
		☐	☐
		☐	☐
		☐	☐
		☐	☐
		☐	☐
		☐	☐
		☐	☐
		☐	☐
		☐	☐

QUIZ

B

MY QUESTION	YOUR ANSWER	RIGHT!	WRONG!
What's my biggest fear?		☐	☐
Who's my celebrity crush?		☐	☐
		☐	☐
		☐	☐
		☐	☐
		☐	☐
		☐	☐
		☐	☐
		☐	☐
		☐	☐
		☐	☐
		☐	☐
		☐	☐
		☐	☐
		☐	☐
		☐	☐
		☐	☐

FUNNY THINGS YOU

A

TEASE ME ABOUT

B

_____

_____

_____

_____

_____

_____

_____

_____

_____

_____

_____

_____

_____

_____

_____

_____

_____

WHAT I LOVE

A

_____

_____

_____

_____

_____

_____

_____

_____

_____

_____

_____

_____

_____

_____

_____

ABOUT YOU

B

_____
_____
_____
_____
_____
_____
_____
_____
_____
_____
_____
_____
_____
_____
_____
_____

COMEDIANS, SPEAKERS, AND OTHER THEATER EVENTS WE'VE SEEN

_____

_____

_____

_____

_____

_____

_____

_____

_____

HAIKUS FOR

EACH OTHER

RESTAURANTS OF
SPECIAL SIGNIFICANCE TO US

CUISINES WE'VE TRIED AND WANT TO TRY

TRIED

TO TRY

☐

☐

☐

☐

☐

☐

☐

☐

☐

☐

☐

☐

☐

TRIED   **TO TRY**

_____   ☐   _____

_____   ☐   _____

_____   ☐   _____

_____   ☐   _____

_____   ☐   _____

_____   ☐   _____

_____   ☐   _____

_____   ☐   _____

_____   ☐   _____

_____   ☐   _____

_____   ☐   _____

_____   ☐   _____

_____   ☐   _____

OUR BEST DATES

_____

_____

_____

_____

_____

_____

_____

_____

_____

_____

_____

_____

_____

_____

_____

_____

_____

_____

_____

_____

OUR DATE NIGHT FAILS

A

ALL—OCCASION APOLOGY

LETTERS TO EACH OTHER

OUR FUNNEST MOMENTS
AND BIGGEST LAUGHS

FIRST IMPRESSIONS

A

_____

_____

_____

_____

_____

_____

_____

_____

_____

_____

_____

_____

_____

_____

_____

_____

_____

_____

OF EACH OTHER

B

_____

_____

_____

_____

_____

_____

_____

_____

_____

_____

_____

_____

_____

_____

_____

THINGS WE HOPE TO
EXPERIENCE TOGETHER

"WHAT WOULD I BE?"

A

	YOUR GUESS	MY ANSWER
Animal		
Flower		
Car		
Song		
Movie		
Actor		
Dessert		
Dog		
Band		
Hashtag		
Season		
Book		
Animated character		
Superhero		
Word		

QUIZ

B

	YOUR GUESS	MY ANSWER
Animal		
Flower		
Car		
Song		
Movie		
Actor		
Dessert		
Dog		
Band		
Hashtag		
Season		
Book		
Animated character		
Superhero		
Word		

CHALLENGES AND EXPERIMENTAL
THINGS WE SHOULD TRY

SMALL HABITS TO TRY
FOR THIRTY DAYS

- [ ] Kisses on the cheek every morning
- [ ] Send one compliment text per day
- [ ]
- [ ]
- [ ]
- [ ]
- [ ]
- [ ]
- [ ]
- [ ]
- [ ]
- [ ]
- [ ]
- [ ]
- [ ]
- [ ]
- [ ]

- [ ] _____
- [ ] _____
- [ ] _____
- [ ] _____
- [ ] _____
- [ ] _____
- [ ] _____
- [ ] _____
- [ ] _____
- [ ] _____
- [ ] _____
- [ ] _____
- [ ] _____
- [ ] _____
- [ ] _____
- [ ] _____
- [ ] _____

TOPICS OF OUR MOST MEMORABLE SQUABBLES

"WOULD YOU STILL LOVE ME IF..."

A

I had a tail?

☐ ☐

☐ ☐

☐ ☐

☐ ☐

☐ ☐

☐ ☐

☐ ☐

☐ ☐

☐ ☐

☐ ☐

☐ ☐

☐ ☐

☐ ☐

☐ ☐

☐ ☐

☐ ☐

☐ ☐

☐ ☐

QUIZ

B

We didn't speak the same language? ☐ ☐

☐ ☐

☐ ☐

☐ ☐

☐ ☐

☐ ☐

☐ ☐

☐ ☐

☐ ☐

☐ ☐

☐ ☐

☐ ☐

☐ ☐

☐ ☐

☐ ☐

☐ ☐

☐ ☐

☐ ☐

CAUSES AND ORGANIZATIONS
WE SUPPORT

THINGS WE NEED TO WORK ON AS A COUPLE

_____

_____

_____

_____

_____

_____

_____

_____

_____

_____

_____

_____

_____

A

I'M SORRY FOR

I FORGIVE YOU FOR

APOLOGY AND

B

I'M SORRY FOR

_____

_____

_____

_____

_____

_____

_____

_____

_____

_____

_____

_____

I FORGIVE YOU FOR

_____

_____

_____

_____

_____

_____

_____

_____

_____

_____

_____

_____

FORGIVENESS PRACTICE

OUR FAVORITE SHOWS

OUR BIGGEST SPLURGES
AND DREAM SPLURGES

SPLURGES

DREAM SPLURGES

_____

HOW WE'VE BEEN INSPIRED BY

A

_____

_____

_____

_____

_____

_____

_____

_____

_____

_____

_____

_____

_____

_____

_____

_____

OR LEARNED FROM EACH OTHER

B

_____

_____

_____

_____

_____

_____

_____

_____

_____

_____

_____

_____

_____

_____

_____

_____

STICK FIGURE COMIC STRIP

ABOUT HOW WE MET

MEMORABLE DETAILS
ABOUT WHEN WE FELL IN LOVE

_____

_____

_____

_____

_____

_____

_____

_____

_____

_____

_____

_____

_____

_____

_____

INDIVIDUAL GOALS

A

AND DREAMS

B

_____

_____

_____

_____

_____

_____

_____

_____

_____

_____

_____

_____

_____

_____

GIFTS WE'VE
GIVEN EACH OTHER

FAVORITE GIFTS TO RECEIVE

A

_____

_____

_____

_____

_____

_____

_____

_____

_____

_____

_____

_____

_____

(HINT HINT)

B

_____

_____

_____

_____

_____

_____

_____

_____

_____

_____

_____

_____

_____

_____

_____

"WHO'S MORE LIKELY TO . . ."

A

	ME	YOU
Fall asleep during a movie?	☐	☐
	☐	☐
	☐	☐
	☐	☐
	☐	☐
	☐	☐
	☐	☐
	☐	☐
	☐	☐
	☐	☐
	☐	☐
	☐	☐
	☐	☐
	☐	☐
	☐	☐
	☐	☐
	☐	☐
	☐	☐

QUIZ

B

	ME	YOU
Trip in public?	☐	☐
	☐	☐
	☐	☐
	☐	☐
	☐	☐
	☐	☐
	☐	☐
	☐	☐
	☐	☐
	☐	☐
	☐	☐
	☐	☐
	☐	☐
	☐	☐
	☐	☐
	☐	☐
	☐	☐
	☐	☐

RECIPES, GAMES, AND OTHER HOME ACTIVITIES TO TRY

- [ ]
- [ ]
- [ ]
- [ ]
- [ ]
- [ ]
- [ ]
- [ ]
- [ ]
- [ ]
- [ ]
- [ ]
- [ ]
- [ ]
- [ ]
- [ ]
- [ ]
- [ ]
- [ ]

REAL AND FICTIONAL
COUPLES WHO INSPIRE US

_____   _____

_____   _____

_____   _____

_____   _____

_____   _____

_____   _____

_____   _____

_____   _____

_____   _____

_____   _____

_____   _____

_____   _____

OUR INDIVIDUAL INSECURITIES

A

_____ _____
_____ _____
_____ _____
_____ _____
_____ _____
_____ _____
_____ _____
_____ _____
_____ _____
_____ _____
_____ _____
_____ _____
_____ _____
_____ _____
_____ _____
_____ _____

THAT REQUIRE TENDERNESS

B

_____   _____

_____   _____

_____   _____

_____   _____

_____   _____

_____   _____

_____   _____

_____   _____

_____   _____

_____   _____

_____   _____

_____   _____

_____   _____

_____   _____

_____   _____

_____   _____

_____   _____

OUR MOST MEMORABLE GETAWAYS AND ADVENTURES

MY FAVORITE STORIES

A

_____

_____

_____

_____

_____

_____

_____

_____

_____

_____

_____

_____

_____

_____

ABOUT YOUR LIFE

B

_____

_____

_____

_____

_____

_____

_____

_____

_____

_____

_____

_____

_____

_____

_____

_____

THINGS WE EACH

A

FEAR

LOVE

_____

_____

_____

_____

_____

_____

_____

_____

_____

_____

_____

_____

_____

_____

_____

_____

_____

_____

FEAR AND LOVE

B

FEAR	LOVE

OUR MOST
ROMANTIC MOMENTS

_____

_____

_____

_____

_____

_____

_____

_____

_____

_____

_____

_____

_____

_____

_____

_____

_____

_____

_____

_____

_____

HOW WE'D
DESCRIBE EACH

A

_____
_____
_____
_____
_____
_____
_____
_____
_____
_____
_____
_____
_____
_____
_____
_____

OTHER TO
OTHER PEOPLE

B

_____

_____

_____

_____

_____

_____

_____

_____

_____

_____

_____

_____

_____

_____

_____

_____

_____

A

MESSAGES TO EACH OTHER

B

IN SONG LYRICS

WHAT WE EACH

A

_____

_____

_____

_____

_____

_____

_____

_____

_____

_____

_____

_____

_____

_____

_____

_____

_____

FIND SEXY

B

_____

_____

_____

_____

_____

_____

_____

_____

_____

_____

_____

_____

_____

_____

_____

NICE THINGS WE'VE DONE
FOR EACH OTHER

HOW WE DREAM OUR LIVES
WILL BE WHEN WE'RE OLD

_____

_____

_____

_____

_____

_____

_____

_____

_____

_____

_____

_____

_____

_____

_____

_____

_____

A

ALL THE WORDS THAT COME

B

TO MIND LOOKING AT EACH OTHER

EVERY FUN THING TO DO IN OUR CITY

"FIRSTS" WE'VE EXPERIENCED TOGETHER

I THINK YOU'RE

A

_____

_____

_____

_____

_____

_____

_____

_____

_____

_____

_____

_____

_____

_____

_____

_____

GOOD AT . . .

B

_____
_____
_____
_____
_____
_____
_____
_____
_____
_____
_____
_____
_____
_____
_____
_____
_____

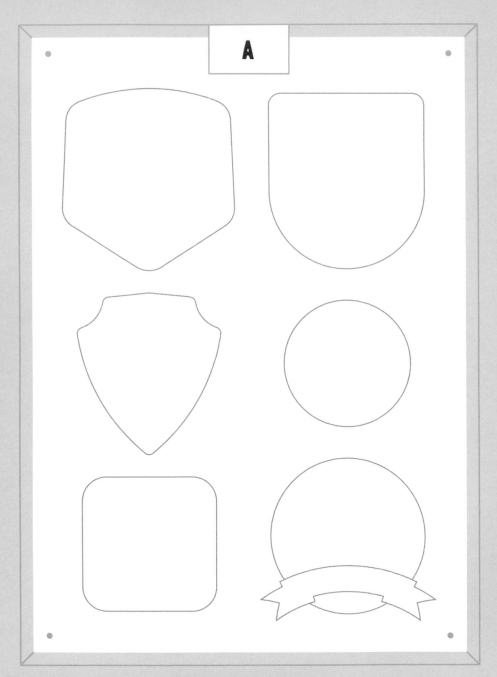

SCOUT BADGES

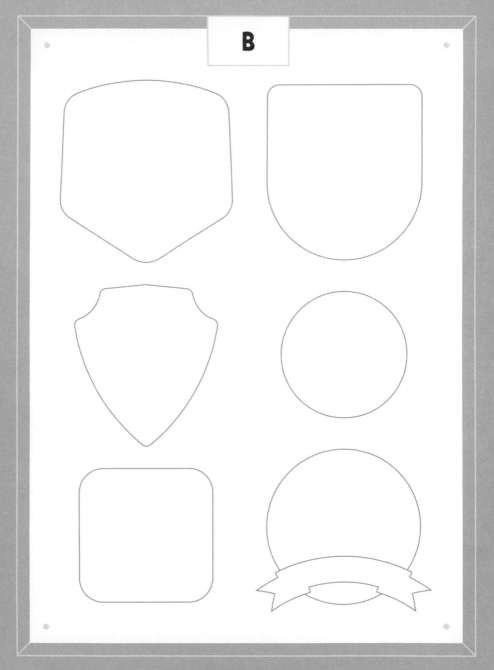

B

WE'VE EARNED

THINGS WE
SHOULDN'T TAKE

A

_____
_____
_____
_____
_____
_____
_____
_____
_____
_____
_____
_____
_____
_____
_____

FOR GRANTED
ABOUT EACH OTHER

B

_____

_____

_____

_____

_____

_____

_____

_____

_____

_____

_____

_____

_____

_____

_____

_____

_____

WHAT WE'D DO WITH ONE LAST DAY ON EARTH

A

HOW TO MAKE ME

B

FEEL LOVED

WEEKEND GETAWAY IDEAS

_____

_____

_____

_____

_____

_____

_____

_____

_____

_____

_____

_____

_____

_____

MUSEUMS WE'VE VISITED AND WANT TO VISIT

VISITED

TO VISIT

_____   ☐   _____
_____   ☐   _____
_____   ☐   _____
_____   ☐   _____
_____   ☐   _____
_____   ☐   _____
_____   ☐   _____
_____   ☐   _____
_____   ☐   _____
_____   ☐   _____
_____   ☐   _____
_____   ☐   _____
_____   ☐   _____
_____   ☐   _____
_____   ☐   _____
_____   ☐   _____

ALL THE QUALITIES

A

_____   _____

_____   _____

_____   _____

_____   _____

_____   _____

_____   _____

_____   _____

_____   _____

_____   _____

_____   _____

_____   _____

_____   _____

_____   _____

_____   _____

OF A GOOD RELATIONSHIP

B

_____

_____

_____

_____

_____

_____

_____

_____

_____

_____

_____

_____

_____

_____

_____

_____

_____

DATE IDEAS

A

A LOVE LETTER

B

FROM EACH OF US

STARTER QUESTIONS

A

☐ _____

☐ _____

☐ _____

☐ _____

☐ _____

☐ _____

☐ _____

☐ _____

☐ _____

☐ _____

☐ _____

☐ _____

☐ _____

☐ _____

☐ _____

☐ _____

☐ _____

FOR DINNER DATES

B

- [ ] _____
- [ ] _____
- [ ] _____
- [ ] _____
- [ ] _____
- [ ] _____
- [ ] _____
- [ ] _____
- [ ] _____
- [ ] _____
- [ ] _____
- [ ] _____
- [ ] _____
- [ ] _____
- [ ] _____
- [ ] _____
- [ ] _____
- [ ] _____

FAVORITE MEMORIES

_____

_____

_____

_____

_____

_____

_____

_____

_____

_____

_____

_____

_____

_____

_____

_____

_____

Create Your Own

Create Your Own

Create Your Own

Create Your Own